Wil

MW01201628

The Family Man's Guide to Basic Preparedness

By Shawn Clay

Introduction

If you are like the average married man with kids, your life does not revolve around preparing for doomsday scenarios. Thoughts of EMP strikes, a zombie apocalypse, destructive acts of nature, or mass civil unrest does not keep you tossing and turning at night. You've got other things that occupy all that grey matter between your ears. There's the mortgage, the doctor bills, the ballgames, the dance recitals, that upcoming anniversary or birthday, and a myriad of other responsibilities that pull us in every conceivable direction. "That's life", you tell yourself, "who has time to worry about stuff down the road that may or may not ever come to pass?" A valid question, to be sure. However, it is one that needs to be addressed. And, as head of your family, it's up to you to address it. My hope is that this book allows you to do just that.

If you were to do a "man on the street" type of interview in any city or town across this nation and ask what a "prepper" was, you would likely get a lot of interesting answers. I would wager to say that most people, when presented with this term, conjure up images of paranoid militia types, holed up in their underground bunkers, surrounded by enough firepower to take out a small nation and freeze-dried food stacked floor to ceiling. It's a perception that most would likely not want to be branded with. I couldn't agree more. The number of books, television shows, and internet sites devoted to this topic are innumerable. Some are well-reasoned with practical application. Some are fringe sites for nut-jobs who find comfort in numbers. So, how do we cut through all the static to find common ground?

Before we get into the practical aspects of the subject, we need to understand some basic principles regarding the concept of prepping. While the current generation may consider prepping to be something to poke fun at or ignore altogether, let's not forget that we are only two or three generations removed from our ancestors who likely incorporated prepping into their lifestyle, even if they had never heard that term. How many of us had grandparents or great-grandparents who farmed or gardened and canned their harvest? Perhaps they raised cows, chickens, pigs, etc. to slaughter. How many of us can remember relatives who knew how to hunt, fish, camp, and live off the land? Perhaps you had ancestors who delivered their own children due to the lack of a doctor in the area. More recently, I can remember my grandfather working on his own cars, far beyond a simple oil change or tire rotation. They never considered any of this "prepping". To them, it was just part of being self-reliant. Some of today's generation cannot grasp the concept that there wasn't a big box grocery / sporting goods / auto care store on every corner 50 or 100 years ago. People had to provide and watch out for themselves and their families. Go back and read accounts of how people weathered the Great Depression for a good take on how this mentality was more than prevalent back then. Our "disposable society" has shifted our outlook from one of self-reliance to one of "I'll just run by Walmart tomorrow and pick that up."

Many readers may be Christians, or at least have a passing familiarity with the bible and its teachings. There are several references to a preparedness mindset found in scripture. Consider Proverbs 22:3 (NIV): "The prudent see danger and take refuge, but the simple keep going and pay the penalty." Another relevant verse is Proverbs 21:20, which states that "the wise store up choice food and olive oil, but fools gulp theirs down." There are countless other examples in scripture as well. Consider the account in Genesis 41 where the Egyptian pharaoh's dream was interpreted by Joseph. He warned the pharaoh that 7 years of famine and hard times were coming, but these 7 years would be preceded by 7 years of abundance. The pharaoh took Joseph's admonition to heart, appointing him to oversee a gargantuan effort to prepare for the trial ahead. All of Egypt went into a preparedness mindset, putting back food and grain for the days to come. Storehouses were built to keep the supplies centralized, and even the animals were accounted for in the preparation plan. The result was that Egypt fared well during the famine, while the surrounding nations became dependent on them for their very survival, as they had not taken similar steps.

By now, it should be clear that the concept of prepping for an uncertain future is by no means a new one. Humans have been doing so for thousands of years and on every corner of the earth. So, what does this mean to this generation and, more specifically, its' men? As men, we are the head of our households. It's tasked to us to properly provide for and ensure the safety of our wives and children. This is not a chauvinistic or "macho" point of view. I realize there are different types of families, and my goal is not to condemn or belittle anything outside the realm of the traditional family, and I would encourage any family unit to consider the importance of planning for the unknown, for the preparedness mindset is not beholden to any one group. However, this book is specifically meant to address a man's duty to his family.

All too often in our modern society, men fall victim to the many demands that pull us in every conceivable direction. As a result, our families often come last. To put it mildly, this is a problem, and most definitely a cause of marital strife. Once again, the bible offers unmistakable instruction on this topic. 1 Timothy 5:8 states that, "Anyone who does not provide for their relatives, and especially for their own household, has denied the faith and is worse than an unbeliever." The message here is simple, guys: family first. Your job, your social life, and your toys should all come in a very distant second place. If your family is taking a backseat to anything else in your life, it's time for some self-evaluation. I cannot stress this enough. Nothing, I repeat, NOTHING comes before your family. I'm firmly convinced that if the men of this generation would act like real men, a lot of society's problems would resolve themselves.

Now that I've preached my sermon for the week, let's get down to business.

Table of Contents

Chapter 1

Getting Started

As stated in the introduction, the word "prepping" causes many different reactions when discussed in public. Discussions can range from casually brushing off the topic (usually with the phrase "like that's ever really going to happen") to heated debates regarding whether or not the AR15 is the ideal weapon for when the SHTF ("Stuff" Hits The Fan – buckle up, there are many interesting terms you'll encounter in the world of prepping). Let me be clear from the start: I'm not an active or former Delta Force, super-secret operator with decades' worth of experience living off the land. I don't play a survival expert on TV who drinks his own pee every time the opportunity presents itself. I don't have a retired missile silo deep underground to retreat to in the event of a nuke strike. If you are looking for advice from folks of that caliber, I'm not your guy. I am, however, a husband to a wonderful wife and a father to a pair of incredible kids. I may not be able to show you how to survive in the post-apocalyptic world where gangs of bandits roam. What I can do, is show you practical steps to ensure that any event, be it major or minor, is a little less intimidating by putting in some basic time preparing for the future. In short, I'm not going to tell you what to do as much as I am going to try and encourage you how to think. Preparedness is more than just gear; it's a mindset.

One need not have a lifestyle consumed with preparing a contingency plan for every single scenario that Murphy may throw at us. Recall my earlier statement of "family first." Far too many well-intentioned guys jump into the world of prepping with both feet, and the concept itself turns into a life-dominating activity. There must be an adequate balance between the prepping mindset and everyday life. Surfing the internet trying to find the best fixed blade knife for your bug out bag instead of spending time reading to your kids is not time well spent. And let me be the first to say that I have been guilty of this one. It's easy to do. Repeat to yourself: "moderation in all things."

Now that you have decided that the half case of bottled water and the 2 cans of spam left over from your last camping trip don't exactly constitute a survival plan, how do you get started down the road to readiness? Surely the answer lies in going into the nearest outdoor / sporting goods store and dropping $10k on survival gear, bringing it home, packing it neatly into storage totes, and shoving it all into the back of the closet, right? Unfortunately, this is a common mistake among beginning preppers. And Heaven knows, we guys like shiny things and are subject to buying it up without really thinking through what we are doing. I will do my best to break things down into a simple, easy to accomplish checklist of the most basic necessities that you should have on hand for both your home and each vehicle under your care.

So, before you run out and buy a satellite phone and a surplus HUMVEE, let's stop and look at the basics of what every household should have on hand. This is by no means an exhaustive list, and we will go into more detail about additional items to keep on hand later in the book. In addition, your circumstances may dictate that you alter or add your own necessities, but the building blocks lie in the following areas:

Water

Food

First Aid

Shelter

Water

Unless you are on well water, you likely find yourself dependent on your city or county water company to supply your homes. Service interruptions can occur at any time, and as the recent situation in Flint, Michigan has shown us, aging or neglected infrastructure can lead to a catastrophic failure of the system overnight. So, imagine that you wake up one random weekday morning and go to turn on the shower and nothing but a trickle of cold water comes out. What do you do now (other than calling the water company's 24 hour helpline and listening to the automated recording assuring you, oh valued customer, that they are diligently working to correct the problem and that you can expect service to be restored sometime between later today and next Friday)?

FEMA (Federal Emergency Management Agency) recommends that all Americans keep a 3 day supply of water and food on hand. They state that you should factor in one gallon of water per person, per day, for both drinking and sanitation purposes. Simply do the math on this one. If you have a wife and 2 children, you will need to keep 12 gallons of water (at a minimum) on hand. To accomplish this, you can buy up the necessary cases of bottled water and set them back (most experts recommend using up and replenishing this supply on a consistent basis) or another option is to purchase several 5 gallon water containers, available in the sporting goods section of most big box stores, and fill them and store them in a cool, dry place. When the seasons change, empty them and refill. This will supply your family with the minimum recommended water to keep on hand. As opportunity allows, continue to expand your emergency water storage. Perhaps a 55 gallon drum designed for potable water is in order, as it will take up minimal space, while providing nearly 5 days of backup water. For all other emergency kits (bug out bags and vehicle kits), only worry about drinking water when factoring in the three day water supply. This will reduce the need to around a half gallon per day.

Food

When it comes to food, there are several different options. There are several companies (Wise Foods, Augason Farms, Mountain House, etc.) that sell pre-packaged, 24-to-72 hour and beyond, freeze dried emergency food kits that have up to a 25-year shelf life. Be aware that these will require water to prepare, so factor that into your water supply. In addition, some of these foods are high in sodium as well. Another popular option is the classic military MRE (meal, ready to eat). These are often found in cases of 12 complete meals and are available in different varieties. Some come with heater tablets to heat the meals. These meals are often labeled with a 5 year shelf life, but are widely known to be safe to eat for many years beyond that date. The third, and possibly most sensible short-term option, is to simply examine your current grocery buying habits.

Most Americans probably go to the grocery store at least once per week. The convenience of being able to pop in for an item or two is something we all too often take for granted. Look in your pantry, and you will likely have enough food to last for 3 days if an event prevented you from being able to get to a grocery store. To ensure that food will not be an issue, you may want to evaluate the possibility of buying groceries every other week or even on a monthly basis. You will find that it often saves time and money to buy in bulk. It need not be more complicated than calculating how many of each item you go through in a week and multiply it by 2 or 4. In addition, many stores like Walmart and Costco offer home delivery of most grocery items, allowing a family to place an order monthly and have the majority of their needs delivered straight to their front door. Items like milk, produce, and fruit are becoming available as well, although you may prefer to pick those up weekly to ensure freshness. Regardless of which method of emergency food you choose, ensure that you replace your reserves if consumed, and monitor items for expiration and consume them beforehand. It would also be wise to have a secondary cooking source. A gas grill or portable camp stove would suffice nicely if your electric stove is down along with the rest of the grid. Most sporting goods stores carry portable stoves that range from single burners to multiple and have various fuel options.

On the subject of buying groceries in bulk, you may want to reconsider how you store food in your home. Rather than trying to cram a month's worth of groceries into your pantry or cabinets, consider if there is a room where you could set up shelving to hold your additional food. A standard 4 foot wide by 6 foot tall shelving unit from any hardware store will likely store both your extra food and emergency water, keeping everything together in a well-organized fashion. I personally have two of these shelving units mounted side by side on the back wall of my garage. I have a one week supply of water in 5 gallon jugs on the bottom of one shelf and a one week supply of bottled water on the other. Every time we drink up one case of bottled water, I pull up the case behind it and replace it the next time we go to the store or get a shipment of groceries in. The remaining shelves hold our extra food, cleaning supplies, toiletries, and paper products (don't forget to order extra paper towels and toilet paper when purchasing monthly; those are two items that you definitely don't want to be without).

First Aid

When it comes to first aid, I would assume most households have a couple boxes of bandages and anti-bacterial cream stashed in various locations. There's also likely a store-bought first aid kit or two lying around as well. While a good start, there is definitely more to being prepared than this. It would be wise to have a dedicated location for all your first aid gear. A cabinet or closet, or even a medic bag, allow you to organize your gear so that you aren't scrambling and searching for that one item you need when time is of the essence. At a bare minimum, I would keep the following on hand for minor first aid emergencies:

Rubbing Alcohol (pads or bottle)

Hydrogen Peroxide

Assorted-sized Bandages

Assorted-sized Gauze Pads

Medical Tape

Medical Wrap / Sterile Pads

Tweezers

Scissors / EMT Shears

Small Flashlight

Aspirin / Ibuprofen (adult and child dosages)

Burn Relief Crème

Anti-bacterial Crème

Bug Bite Relief Crème

Disposable Ice Packs

Stomach / Heartburn Relief Medication

Quick Clot blood stopping kit

Minor surgical kit (scalpel, forceps, etc.)

Thermometer

Splint (limb size and finger size)

All of these items would fit easily into a box or other portable carrying method. Be sure to check medications periodically to ensure that they haven't expired. Most big-box retailers have generic versions of name-brand medications at a substantial discount, so keep an eye out for bargains. While the above list is a good start, there are many other items that you may want to keep on hand. Your situation will be your own, and any other considerations such as Epi-pens, asthma-relief inhalers, insulin for diabetes, etc. will need to be factored in to your planning. Also, when considering medications that you take daily, it would be wise to have a sufficient supply of it on hand as well. Many pharmacies will allow you to choose a three month supply option when refilling medication. Ordering in a larger quantity will stack the deck in your favor, should the supply lines go down during an emergency.

In addition, first aid is more than just having the right supplies on hand. Would you know how to treat a deep laceration from your child accidentally breaking a window? How about a broken bone resulting from a fall from the backyard treehouse? What if your child begins choking at the dinner table? Moments like these, although rare, are going to require that you maintain a level head and know how to react. Organizations such as the American Red Cross offer first aid / CPR certification classes many times per year. They are available at your local chapter and are also often found at area schools, churches, businesses, etc. You would be wise to check and see if your employer offers this training, as it will likely be free of charge. The skills learned over the few hours comprising these courses can truly be life-saving and the content is presented in a very understandable format. Additional advanced training is also available. If time allows, you may check to see if your local EMT service provides training and volunteer opportunities. The best way to stay current is to put those skills into action.

Your level of necessary first aid preparedness will depend on many factors. Consider your level of activity. Do your kids play sports? Does your family spend lots of time outside hiking, camping, etc.? In cases like this, some basic wilderness medical training would be very beneficial. Setting a broken bone, treating an animal bite, preventing shock due to exposure to the elements, etc. are just some of the scenarios that you should probably give some consideration to before that next trek outdoors. Remember, Murphy doesn't confine himself to the four walls of your home by any means.

Shelter

When it comes to the subject of shelter, this can take on many forms. Most of the time, the environment will dictate your response. For our purposes, I will break this down into two parts: shelter in place and shelter on the go.

In most cases, it's obvious that your home will be your most effective form of shelter. However, there are certain precautions that should be taken here as well. In the event of a natural disaster, the local power grid will most likely be down. Do you have alternative methods to heat and cool your home? Portable heaters or battery-powered fans can turn a miserable experience into a tolerable one. A portable generator would allow you to operate certain appliances and possibly the heating / air conditioning system. Should your home become slightly damaged, do you have the means and ability to secure it and keep it habitable? Some tarps tucked away in the garage will go a long way if the roof is damaged or a window blown out by a storm. It would be prudent to be well versed in how to shut off the water, electricity, and gas should an event such as an earthquake cause leaks in your home. It's said that a man's home is his castle, and knowing how to keep it safe and secure will go a long way psychologically towards weathering a disaster, particularly for children. Familiarity and security are very important factors for them.

Some events, however, will necessitate leaving one's home. This could be due to a mandatory evacuation in the event of a chemical spill, flood, wildfire, etc. In events like this, there are a myriad of shelter options. The most obvious would be to simply stay with local friends or relatives, or rent a hotel room for the duration of the event. If this is not an option due to a wide-reaching event, you may be forced to take shelter in your vehicle or another makeshift shelter. In this scenario, a family-size camping tent would be worth its weight in gold. In a pinch, a quality tarp strung up between some trees can keep rain and blistering sun off your loved ones. Consider all the options when deciding how to shelter outside the home. A vehicle can provide hot or cold air for as long as the fuel holds out. Larger trucks and SUV's often have seats that will fold down, allowing for room to stretch out and sleep. They also provide the best protection from the elements. A quality tent would also be a much-preferred choice to roughing it under the stars. If you see that an evacuation is imminent, think through the various options and proceed with the one that will afford the least disruption to your family. As in all of the situations discussed, the appropriate gear is only part of the equation. The second part is you keeping a level and calm demeanor. Projected confidence is going to be a major factor in getting your loved ones through whatever situation you are facing. If you panic, everything falls apart. Dig deep for that ability to compartmentalize, because your family is going to be looking to you for guidance. They need that steady hand and reassuring tone that you will take care of them until things return to normal.

One final note before we begin to delve into other areas and concepts of preparedness: what do you carry on yourself every day that may be useful in an emergency? Have you ever considered what items may be critical to have in arm's reach whenever the unexpected occurs? While I'm not advocating that you walk around with the equivalent of Batman's utility belt strapped around your waist at all times, there are some things that you might want to work into your daily wardrobe.

To keep is simple, I like to carry a pocket knife and a small flashlight at a minimum. While at work, since discretion is key, I carry a small

SOG Micron II folding knife in my pocket. It's very slim and compact and disappears in my pocket until needed. When discretion is not an issue, I carry my Benchmade Griptilian folding knife with pocket clip. Either knife is always complimented by a small Streamlight Nano flashlight. It stays on my keyring and, although quite tiny, it casts a nice beam for its size. Other folks prefer to take it a step further and have some sort of multi-tool on them as well, such as a Swiss Army Knife or a Leatherman tool. While I don't have one on me at all times, one or both of these is in my vehicle in easy reach, along with a larger flashlight.

While a knife definitely comes in handy for all sorts of utilitarian purposes throughout the day from cutting a loose string on your shirt to opening boxes of printer paper, it can also be pressed into a defensive role if needed. The flashlight's benefit is obvious in that it can provide illumination should the power go out, not to mention being able to see under the vending machine when that last quarter slips and invariably rolls underneath it out of sight.

For these daily carry items, look around for what's best for your daily needs. I also carry a small Classic model Swiss Army Knife on my keyring next to the flashlight. It has a main blade, scissors, nail file, toothpick, and tweezers, all in a compact knife that's smaller than a pack of gum. Once you get in the habit of carrying them every day, it becomes second nature. When it comes to other items, get creative in your carry method. For instance, while it's not practical to carry a first aid kit on my person at all times, I can still slide several band aids into one of the pockets of my wallet to have on hand for minor injuries such as a paper cut or a puncture. The less of a hassle something is to carry, the more likely you'll have it on you when you most need it.

Chapter 2

What Are You Preparing For?

Now that we've established the basics that apply to every form of prepping, it only makes sense to take a good look at what we are preparing FOR. In order to develop an action plan, let's focus on these three factors:

Likelihood of an event

Location

Length of time affected

Likelihood of an event – When considering an emergency action plan, you need to first ask yourself what the most likely scenario you will be encountering is. Barring events such as an EMP or massive solar flare taking the power grid down for good, or a nuclear strike from a rogue nation, the list of possible scenarios to plan for should be fairly reasonable. For instance, families in the Midwest will likely rank a tornado or snowstorm as their principle factor in developing an emergency plan, whereas families living in Florida or other coastal states will be contending with hurricanes and the resulting storm surge-induced inland flooding. Families in the southwest may have to plan for heat waves and wildfires due to arid conditions. Families located within the proximity of a power plant (nuclear or otherwise) should be aware of the current evacuation routes. There is no one size fits all scenario to develop an actionable emergency plan, but a little bit of studying your geographic area should allow you to pinpoint the most likely threats to your family's safety. While any area of the nation is subject to shifting and sometimes unprecedented weather events, it would be advisable to pick out the top two or three events that would have the greatest probability of occurring and develop one's action plan from that basis.

Location – Your next consideration when forming your emergency action plan is your physical location. If you are in a flood-prone region, how soon will the water be at your doorstep? If you are in tornado alley, does your home have a basement or somewhere to seek shelter as the storm approaches? If you live in an area prone to wildfires, are you located right next to a forest? Factors such as these can allow you to better formulate an action plan in regards to your response to an emergency situation. Other factors can include whether or not you are in a rural setting or right smack dab in the middle of a large city. Will you be stuck in a sea of panicked people trying to escape a coming storm or will you be all by yourself when the event hits? Once again, there are a myriad of variables to consider regarding your current physical location. An in-depth evaluation should help you make an informed decision regarding your reaction to the threats you deem most probable.

Length of Time Affected – Lastly, you should consider how long you and your family will likely be affected by the event you are preparing to endure. This is where the basics of food, water, first aid, and shelter will play the largest role. If it's a temporary disruption and your main residence is still intact and safe, it may very well make the most sense to simply weather it out where you are. If the disaster had a massive scope of impact, the power will be out and likely weeks away from being restored. Water service may be disrupted as well. In situations like this, it's more likely the wise move to relocate to temporary lodging while order is restored. Unless you are able to ensure that your family is safely out of the elements and can produce your own power, water, etc., it's advisable to move everyone to a more settled environment. Disasters can unfortunately bring out the worst in some people. We've all seen the footage of stores being looted in the aftermath of major storms. Don't let the safety of your family be compromised by staying in a situation that has seen a breakdown of law and order. Your belongings can be replaced. Your loved ones cannot.

Chapter 3

The Psychological Component

As I've mentioned before, a lot of prepping is mental. While it's easy enough to assemble all the right gear, if you're not prepared for an emergency mentally, then you are severely handicapped from the outset. The man of the house needs to project an air of confidence and stability, not only during times of emergency but in the day to day grind as well. The emotions in the build-up and the aftermath of an emergency can vary wildly in your loved ones. Children may cry, not be able to sleep, display anger, etc. If you are anything like me, your spouse is the dynamo that keeps your house moving. She will likely look to you for guidance and assurance that it's all going to be OK. In short, now is not the time for you to break down into a blubbery mess.

If you and your family are new to prepping, the change may bring about apprehension, especially in children. I know when I began to get a little more serious about things, my young children would ask why I was doing whatever it was I was doing or assembling at the time. I simply explained to them that I was getting things together that would help us if we ever had an emergency. I tried to calm any fears that something was imminent by pointing out that being prepared at home is just like wearing a seatbelt in the car. You don't ever expect a wreck to happen, but you certainly want to be prepared should one occur. My area of North Georgia experienced a major storm system that spawned numerous tornados back in April of 2011. My children listened all day to the warning sirens blaring as the next cell approached. We were blessed in that our immediate surroundings were spared. Other families just a few miles down the road were not so fortunate. To say that I was terrified was an understatement. However, when two scared children are looking to you for reassurance, I had to shut that down and remain level-headed.

That experience also served to show that I had several gaps in what I thought was a pretty comprehensive emergency plan. Our house has only a crawlspace, so no basement was available during the tornado outbreak. We did the best we could and cleared out the space under our stairs and used that as our storm shelter. A quick look at the homes that were decimated showed just how much of a gamble that truly was. In addition, I had a small gas-powered generator at the time and thought that I would be just fine. It turned out that the generator was barely capable of running a few appliances at a time. There were several lessons learned. As a result, I installed a steel safe room in my garage that only takes up a 6x9 foot area, yet has plenty of room for my whole family, including pets, and is rated to withstand an F5 rated storm. I also purchased a larger standby generator that turns on automatically, runs off my underground propane tank, and is capable of powering the whole house.

The after effects of an event can definitely shape a child's outlook on life. My son still gets extremely nervous when a major storm system is brewing. I've shown him my shelter, and while is certainly doesn't negate all his fears, it allows him to understand that even though a tornado is extremely scary, our family has a place to go to stay safe. The ability to remain calm and field the same questions repeatedly (such as: "Dad, its dark outside. I'm afraid a tornado is coming." Or "Daddy, what If _____ happens? What will we do???") will help you, as a father, to bring down the anxiety level a few notches.

If you are forced to evacuate, you need to have a mental game plan for your return. I would advise that you and your spouse prepare yourself for the worst case scenario. Be ready for tears, anger, yelling, etc., if you arrive home and your house is completely destroyed. The grief and sense of loss will be overpowering. Again, this is one of those times you have to be your family's solid ground. Deal with things on a minute by minute basis in the beginning. Push back your own feelings of panic, despair, etc. and listen to their fears and worries. Be that shoulder to cry on when everything's gone. Sometimes you might just have to sit in silence and console your family. As the man of the house, you do whatever it takes for however long it takes to guide your family through this. As a Christian, I find that my faith is my strongest ally during trying times. It keeps me going and gives me a source of strength to draw from. It's going to be a time of trial, but a little mental preparation on the front end will help you be what you need to be for your family if that time ever comes. Research how soldiers in the military are taught to compartmentalize and attempt to put that into practice. It's one of the most valuable tools that a prepper can have in their arsenal.

If you can, encourage your children and spouse to play an active role in prepping as well. Make it a family activity. Anything that reduces the stigma or fear associated with it will be advantageous for you, and it will hopefully help them rationalize in their own minds that just because you are taking these steps, doesn't mean that something is imminent. Rather, your goal is to shape their thinking into one of "dad is doing what he needs to do to make sure we're OK if an emergency happens." Preparedness is about facing an uncertain future with confidence and planning, not ignoring it and hoping it never happens to you.

Chapter 4

The Financial Component

Let's face it guys: we love our toys. A quick trip to any major outdoor superstore will convince any man that he REALLY does need that new bass boat or ATV, and heaven help us if we drive by the local truck dealership when the new models come out. Better yet, take 60, 72, even 84 months to pay it off! No down payment and a free Visa gift card with purchase! Impulse purchasing has ruined many a man's marriage and has led to some men working countless hours to pay for toys that they no longer have time to enjoy.

Now, I don't begrudge any man the ability to enjoy the fruits of his labor, but if you are financing a truck, boat, hunting club membership, ATV, and the newest zero-turn lawn mower, then it's time to step back a little and evaluate those pesky things I like to refer to as "priorities". Being guilty myself of most of the stupid ways to wind up in debt, I am now a huge proponent of the Dave Ramsey mentality. In short, he teaches that if you cannot pay for something up front with cash, you can't afford it. Just because you can make the payments is not justification for buying that new _____. What happens if you lose that cushy job with all the perks? Are there savings in the bank that are ready and willing to carry you through until you find another job? Is it really worth financing something for nearly a decade and carrying around that payment like it's a family pet?

It should come as no shock that the prepping mindset should also be present in our financial planning. After all, aren't we taught to "put back for a rainy day"? I would wager to say that most of us put back a percentage of our pay into a company-sponsored 401k or some other form of a retirement fund. That is a great first step, but there are other factors that need to be considered as well.

Let's imagine the scenario described above. The company you've worked for the last 10 years is bought out by another and you show up on Monday morning to find that your services are no longer required. What then? How soon will that new truck and boat be the property of the finance company? Studies have shown that far too many American households live paycheck to paycheck. One slight disruption and the whole illusion of "I can afford it" crumbles like a house of cards. I drive a 2000 model Chevrolet Z71 pickup. It's dented and dinged, but in excellent mechanical condition. Best of all, it's PAID FOR. It will also do everything that a new truck will do, minus a lovely GPS voice telling me where to turn or enhancing my auditory experience with the finest stereo system available. I readily admit that it's tough to not drool as I pass by the Chevrolet and Ford dealerships near me, but that intense feeling of wanting to stop is quickly tempered by the thought of a $600 per month truck payment.

The financial component of prepping is very straight forward: eliminate as much debt as possible and save for the future. Now it's decision time. If you can afford to pay off that auto loan, it would be wise to do so. If not, it may be time to look at downgrading to a more affordable vehicle. The same goes for all the other causes of non-essential monthly expenses. Paying off all debt except your mortgage results in an incredible amount of breathing room, not only in your bank account, but in your overall stress level as well.

Take a look at credit cards as well. I would wager to say that most guys carry at least a marginal balance on them, with some men being maxed out every month. If you have the discipline to use a credit card and pay off the balance in full every month, then you likely will be OK. If you are like me, you're better off without them. I made the decision to get rid of every credit card I owned a while back. It's definitely made me more cognizant of my spending, as that debit card is a little harder to pull out than the Visa from the mega-sporting goods store that earns me points towards future purchases. It also forces me to watch every single dollar.

Once debt is paid off, it's time to start looking down the road. Again, Mr. Ramsey suggests keeping a 3-6 month emergency fund that will cover all of your normal weekly and monthly expenses. On top of that, he recommends putting 15% of your income into a retirement account. Your journey to becoming debt free may vary from what I have detailed here, but being as free as possible from lenders will only help to enhance your ability to prepare for the future and make the necessary investments into your family's safety. Again, scripture contains valuable instruction in this area. Consider the words of Proverbs 22:7 – "The rich rule over the poor, and the borrower is slave to the lender". If you have a spending / saving problem, be man enough to address it. Just as exercise and good eating habits can prevent future health problems, having little-to-no debt and money in the bank can prevent a lot of life's unforeseen financial problems.

Chapter 5

The Physical Component

As I alluded to in the previous chapter, physical fitness plays an important role in the world of prepping. All too often, preppers with good intentions will attend to every aspect of the concept except for the physical aspect. To be fair, very few of us guys are ready to compete in the next Ironman competition, but all of us should aspire to a basic level of health and fitness. After all, how do you expect to lead your family to safety in the event that you are required to bug out on foot if you can't even make it past the mailbox while wearing your bug out bag?

While getting in shape can often be viewed as a daunting task, it really can be done quite simply if one just applies himself. First things first: get a physical from your primary physician. Most insurance plans cover the cost of an annual physical, so that's one less excuse you have for getting one. By doing so, your doctor can diagnose potential issues and, if necessary, begin the process of treatment or management. There's simply no good reason not to have an annual physical.

During your physical, your doctor will no doubt point out what most of us already know: we could stand to lose a little weight. Again, this need not be cause for panic. Simply eliminating the fast food diet that most of us partake in will pay huge dividends in the long run, both financially and physically. The benefits from eliminating the foods that harm the body and replacing them with healthy choices are myriad. Some problems, such as diabetes, heart disease, and high blood pressure, can all be reduced or in some cases, eliminated, by proper diet and exercise.

When forming an emergency plan, we know that one option that needs to be considered is that of having to bug out on foot. Being physically fit will pay off huge if this is the case. You will be better suited to face an uncertain world. Being fit will allow your body to stay off medications, which may have very limited availability during a disaster. Being fit will also allow you to be more flexible, thereby reducing injuries due to over-exertion. Your immune system will operate more efficiently, which is vitally important in a scenario where hygiene services are reduced or non-existent.

Lastly, being fit is going to put you back in the game when it comes to having fun with your family. Family outings such as hiking and camping can incorporate both exercise and preparedness all in one activity. There's really no disadvantage to transitioning to a healthier lifestyle, and those changes very well may be the deciding factor in surviving an extended disaster, be it natural or man-made. Start slow, and build up over time. It won't be long until the soreness and pain begins to subside, and your body begins its' transition back to those college days when you were in the best shape of your life. Not to mention that your spouse will undoubtedly look at you differently as you begin to shed all those unwanted pounds.

Chapter 6

Vehicles

When one thinks about a bugout vehicle, there are probably certain images that come to mind: jacked-up trucks with campers on the back, armor-clad HUMVEES, and everyone's favorite, the deuce-and-a-half military transport truck. While these vehicles certainly have merit, most of us don't have one sitting in the driveway, and it's certainly NOT my intention to suggest that anyone go out and buy something simply in the name of "prepping" (I can hear it now: "but the guy who wrote the book said I NEEDED to go out and buy the new 2017 F-450 with every available option......").

The point of this chapter is to go out in your garage or driveway and examine the vehicle (s) parked there and ask yourself if they are roadworthy enough for a bugout scenario, be it temporary or long term. If you, as most American families do, have more than one vehicle, I would suggest designating one as the primary evacuation vehicle and form some of your emergency plan around it. More than likely, this will be the "family" vehicle that you take on trips, etc. Generally, it will be the roomiest vehicle in your fleet as well.

Once you have designated which vehicle will be your dedicated evacuation vehicle, ask yourself if you know how to perform the basic maintenance required to keep it running. Can you change the oil? Can you replace the radiator hose? Change out a burned-out headlight, replace a busted serpentine belt, clean corrosion off the battery terminals, etc.? Some newer cars are nearly impossible to work on, a truth revealed the first time I tried to change the oil on my wife's then relatively new Honda car. I determined that in order to access the oil filter, my arm would need to bend in about 3 more places that I had the natural ability to bend. In cases such as these, following the manufacturer's recommended maintenance schedule to the best of your ability will be your best bet. If your vehicle is of the type that you can do minor to major repairs yourself, I would obtain a print version of the factory owner's manual if it is not present, and also one of the aftermarket repair manuals, such as the ones that Chilton or Haynes produce. Knowing the mechanics of your vehicle inside and out will help you keep it going when you need to rely on it the most. Preventive maintenance can be the difference between getting back on the road and simply waiting for help. Wiper blades, batteries, belts, and hoses will often fail at the most inopportune time. Make sure that everything is in proper working order at all times. If not, correct or repair the issue in the quickest possible time frame. I put off replacing my windshield wiper motor on an old mudding truck of mine one time. That definitely saved me some money in the short term. It also nearly got me killed the first time a good rain came along.

It would also be advisable that everyone of driving age know how to do the basics as well. They may not be able to replace a headlight or remove an idler pulley, but they definitely need to know how to check the oil, transmission fluid, antifreeze, etc., as well as how to change a flat tire and the proper location for securing a tow rope. Having multiple people with knowledge of your vehicle will be advantageous not only during emergencies, but also during that late night flat tire on the side of the road in the middle of nowhere.

In keeping with the preparedness mindset, an emergency kit should also be present not only in your officially-designated evacuation vehicle, but in every other vehicle in your possession as well. Items I would include would be:

Emergency Drinking Water (I prefer the Datrex brand pouches)

Small water purifier (Lifestraw, SteriPEN, iodine tablets, etc.)

Emergency Food (I chose the 5-year shelf life Datrex emergency ration bars)

Small tool kit (hammer, screwdrivers, pliers, socket set, hose clamps, zip ties)

Quality first aid kit

Flashlight (with extra batteries)

Road flares

Small automotive fire extinguisher

Blanket

Cell phone charger

Tire gauge

Tire Sealant (I like Fix-a-flat personally)

Jumper Cables

Gloves

One roll each of duct tape and electrical tape

Tow strap or tow rope

Utility tool (Leatherman, Swiss Army Knife, etc.)

Poncho (roadside issues love to happen during a good downpour)

Ice Scraper

Small folding shovel

All of these items will fit well in a small plastic tote or duffle bag / backpack and can be kept in the trunk or some other inconspicuous place until needed. I keep a kit in the trunk of each of our cars and one under the rear seat of my truck. It should be noted that any food and medication stored in the kit should be rotated out as the expiration date is passed.

If space allows, there are two other items that I like to keep in my vehicles and would advise others to do as well. One is a combination air compressor and jump start unit. The one I keep in my truck also has two standard electrical outlets to plug into as well. It takes up minimal space and is great for boosting someone off in a parking lot, boosting off a riding mower, airing up a leaking tire, etc. My jump starter / compressor has come to the rescue so many times that it's earned a permanent place in my daily driver.

The second optional item I would recommend is a bag of cat litter to aid in getting one unstuck. I can speak from personal experience that this incredible, clay-like concoction can work wonders in getting unstuck from those times when "don't worry, I'm sure the ground isn't THAT wet down there……" Simply pour some in the front and rear of the tire(s) most stuck and let it sit for a few minutes. You should be able to drive right out afterwards. I never believed it until I tried it myself. Now a 20 pound bag of dollar store cat litter rides in my truck tool box at all times.

When it comes to tires, make sure that you keep yours inflated to the recommended pressure listed on the door jamb of your vehicle or in the owner's manual. Make sure the tread depth on your tires is adequate for daily driving and replace them as necessary. Ensure that your vehicle is equipped with the factory jack, tire tool, and spare tire, and that the spare tire is inflated to the proper factory specifications. There's nothing worse than having a flat, only to find that your spare is flat as well. Know how to change your tire in advance. As I stated earlier, sitting on a country road at night or at rush hour on a busy interstate is no time to be consulting the owner's manual for the first time. Practice it once or twice and you should be good to go for when the real thing happens.

It should be noted that there is an ever-expanding world of aftermarket accessories to make our vehicles into whatever we want them to be. Lift kits and winches add further capability to four wheel drive vehicles, and programmable chips can enhance the gas mileage or add incredible horsepower to muscle cars. While there is nothing wrong with customizing your vehicle to fit your preferences or lifestyle, ensure that whatever modifications you make do not set you up for eventual problems down the road. Always have modifications installed correctly and to the manufacturer's specifications.

While most vehicles now have some sort of GPS navigation system, as well as most smart phones, it would still be a good idea to keep a good, old-fashioned road atlas in your vehicle. If the grid is down, or solar flares are inhibiting satellite reception, having a manual way to plan your journey is a worthwhile endeavor. Better yet, print out or write down all of your potential destinations and keep them inside the atlas for quick reference.

Finally, since no vehicle is going anywhere without gas, it should be noted that your vehicle's fuel system should be maintained as well. A quality bottle of fuel system cleaner twice a year should keep all the deposits that like to form from causing any problems. When it comes to selecting what grade gas to run in your vehicle, once again, consult the owner's manual. It's advisable to keep a minimum of half a tank of gas in your vehicle at all times. In places such as Florida, when a hurricane is imminent, one will invariably see interstates packed with vehicles fleeing the path of the storm. Times like this are not when you want to notice that the "low fuel" light just popped on. I also keep several five gallon cans full of fuel on hand for my vehicles as well. If the power is out, your local gas station won't be able to run the pumps. It's a good idea to have enough spare gas to fill your vehicle's tank up on hand at all times. Since most gas now has ethanol in it, I would advise rotating your emergency stock monthly if at all possible, as some gas begins to break down after 30 days or so. Non-ethanol gas is a little pricier, but will keep for longer between rotations. Adding a fuel stabilizer such as Stabil will help lengthen the usable service life of your fuel reserves as well.

Chapter 7

Bugging In

Among the experienced prepping community, a great deal of focus is placed on long-term survival. While definitely a consideration for all preppers, the beginner should focus much more on the short term events that may disrupt his or her life. A solid plan for weathering a short term (a month or less) event will likely cover the majority of issues that a family will potentially face, while also providing a firm foundation and understanding of the prepping philosophy should further planning be required or desired.

Probably the most often debate topic encountered on prepping websites and blogs is the concept of "bugging out". In this often-romanticized view, we picture ourselves and our families escaping the collapse of civilization, carrying only what we need in our bug out bags, as we head to the hills to establish a new life. While fun to think about and mull over, this scenario is really the exception, and should be regarded as an option of last resort. Most situations requiring you to put your prepping skills to work will be of the short term variety. So, before you go abandoning your house and heading for the hills, let's discuss why that may be the absolute worst thing that you can do.

There are a myriad of reasons that one should consider "bugging in", or choosing to stay in one's residence rather than evacuate. Mother Nature, being the unpredictable cuss that she is, can quickly whip up a blizzard in the northwest, trapping people in their houses with only the supplies they have on hand to carry them through. Perhaps you live in a rural mountainous region, and the only road in and out of town has just been taken out by a massive mudslide. Maybe you live in the middle of a large metropolitan area that has just broken out in massive civil unrest due to a court decision.

Protesters have taken to the streets and are fighting with law enforcement, creating a very dangerous situation for a family to be caught up in. As you can see, there are many reasons that staying in place and hunkering down may be your wisest decision. FEMA has even taken the concept of bugging in a step farther and published an official list of what they deem necessary in a home emergency kit. The following list was taken from the FEMA website (the direct link is provided in the back of the book):

Water – one gallon per person, per day for a minimum of 3 days for drinking and sanitation purposes. I personally have a device called a Waterbob that goes in my largest bathtub and secures a hose to the faucet, allowing me to fill the bladder with extra water that can be used to bathe, drink, wash clothes, etc. I keep two on hand so that I can fill both of my bathtubs, extending my water supplies even further.

Food – a minimum 3 day supply of non-perishable food, ideally foods that require minimal or no preparation.

Emergency Radio with NOAA Weather feature – these come in both battery powered and hand crank versions, some of which have cell phone charging capability as well. Make sure to include extra batteries as well.

Flashlight (s) – quality, high lumen flashlight and / or lantern. As with the radio, ensure that extra batteries are present as well.

First Aid Kit – this should be separate from your standard home first aid kit. It will be likely be smaller in size, but ensure that the basics are included as described previously.

Signal whistle – this can be used to signal for help if part of your home has collapsed and you are trapped in the debris or to get the attention of first responders for an injured party.

Dust mask, duct tape and plastic sheeting – to secure against contaminated air.

Toilet paper, garbage bags and a 5 gallon bucket with lid – for personal sanitation. I like the Coleman brand camp wipes. They are great for wiping off and helping your family feel clean while saving water for drinking or cooking purposes. The bags / bucket can be used for sanitation purposes if necessary.

Tool Kit – to include pliers or a wrench to turn off utilities.

Manual can opener – if your choice of food is of the canned variety.

Local maps – in case you need to leave the immediate area for help once the event is over.

Extra prescription medication and glasses – in case your primary medication or glasses are lost or unreachable.

Infant formula and diapers – if applicable.

Pet food and extra water – if applicable.

Copies of important family documents – such as birth certificates, insurance policies, social security info, car titles, mortgage / bank info, and personal identification in a waterproof container or on a flash drive.

Emergency Cash and Coins – keep a few hundred dollars in small bills should you need to seek shelter in a hotel, etc. as ATM's may be unavailable.

Emergency Manuals – first aid, survival manuals, etc.

Sleeping bag or warm blanket – one for each family member.

Change of clothes, including shoes – one for each family member.

Household bleach and medicine dropper – can be used as a disinfectant and to treat water using 16 drops of regular household bleach per gallon of water.

Fire Extinguisher – I would recommend one per floor.

Matches or other fire-starting device – in a secure, waterproof container.

Personal hygiene items – deodorant, toothpaste, toothbrush, floss, body wipes, feminine supplies. The travel size versions are perfect.

Mess kits, paper cups and plates, plastic utensils, paper towels – for preparing emergency foods.

Paper and pen / pencil

Activities for children – books, games, puzzles, etc.

While seemingly an extensive amount of gear, the FEMA recommendations can easily be stored in a couple of large totes, available from any home improvement or big box store. Once assembled, they should be kept in your shelter or whatever room you designate as your gathering point in case of an emergency. Now that you know the minimum to keep on hand in your home, how do we go about bugging in should the situation call for it? A lot of that answer depends on what event is causing you to shelter in place.

If we are looking at a weather-related scenario, your first response is to ensure that your residence is secure and to evaluate any damage that has taken place. If high winds from a passing tornado have damaged your roof, now is the time to get those tarps from the garage and cover the damaged section before beginning the cleanup inside. Now would also be the time to check on neighbors and loved ones in your immediate area. EMS and fire crews may be temporarily unavailable, so ensure that all immediate threats (such as gas lines, downed power lines, etc.) are dealt with appropriately.

Once the situation somewhat stabilizes, it's time to get down to business.

If you happen to have thought ahead and purchased or installed a generator, you will want to cut off all non-essential processes that consume excess power. If you're the only one in your immediate area with backup power, you may become the neighborhood command center. I remember that in the aftermath of an ice storm a few years back, there were only a handful of people in my neighborhood that had backup power supplies. Our houses became the hub where people brought food to keep cool and used our outlets to charge cell phones, lap top computers, etc. Everyone working together will help restore a sense of "normal" to those affected. In addition, keeping busy with things will help keep people's minds, especially children's, off of what has happened and focused on getting everything put back together (sometimes the distraction of an IPad or portable DVD player is just what the doctor ordered).

It's also in a situation like this that having the proper basic emergency essentials set back will pay off in droves, and your storage amounts are only limited by your imagination (or available space). Food can be used to feed not only your family, but also neighbors who were affected. Water supplies can be used for everything from drinking to bathing and keeping plumbing going. First aid supplies and medical training can come into play if there are injured in the immediate area and no EMS crews are available. It's easy to see how bugging in can be advantageous, due to the fact that all of your gear, supplies, etc. do not have to be relocated and can be utilized as needed. In addition, the importance of the ability to maintain as normal an existence as possible cannot be overstated, especially for children. While it's clear that bugging in can have advantages not only for your family, but your immediate community as well, there is another scenario to consider in regards to bugging in.

Now that we've covered the weather-related scenario, let's revisit the social unrest scenario. How many times have we seen a city become a powder keg of raw emotion as a particularly controversial court decision is handed down? Within minutes, riots erupt and violence is widespread. In this situation, making a run for it with your family could have dire consequences. So what do you do in the meantime? Barring any immediate physical threats to your location (building fire, etc.), it may make the most sense to shelter in place and ride it out.

If this is the case, then your approach will be markedly different than the weather-related scenario discussed above. Let's assume you live in an apartment building in the epicenter of the chaos. Your first order of business would be to secure your residence as best as you can. Lock all doors and windows and consider moving your family into an interior room. With any luck, the situation will hopefully resolve itself in 24-48 hours, in which case, you should be fine, assuming you keep a level head. Keep noise to a minimum to avoid attracting attention to your location. Consider covering windows to keep light from emanating out after dark. If the unthinkable happens, and you find your residence under attack, a pre-determined self-defense strategy will come into play. Your conscience will have to be your guide on this matter. There are options that range from non-lethal force up to and including lethal force, such as firearms. Whichever option you choose, ensure that you are properly trained on the legalities of self-defense and use of force. I can think of nothing worse than surviving an ordeal such as this, only to be drug through the court system because, during a few intense seconds of terror, you acted outside the acceptable boundaries of the law. With any luck, your situation will not escalate to this level and the authorities will quell the violence in a short period of time. Once order is restored, you can resume your regular life. However, you must be willing to stand and defend your family if necessary. As I said above, your conscience will have to be your guide on this, and I recommend training with whatever weapon system (lethal or non-lethal) that you choose to employ. Your family needs to know that you are ready and willing to fight to the death to protect them. There is no room for fear or hesitation here. I can think of no more formidable force than a well-equipped father standing between a threat and his family.

To sum up, it's easy to see why having the proper provisions and mindset in place before an event are absolutely essential to successfully surviving an encounter where you are required to shelter in place temporarily. There may be times when you are building your supplies that you think to yourself that you may be overreacting a bit. But when it all hits the fan, I don't know of anyone that would say they were sorry that they had prepped for such an event.

Chapter 8

Bugging Out

Bugging out: it's the stuff of prepper's websites, blogs, and dinner table discussion. More ink and keyboard strokes have probably been devoted to this one topic than all others. It's that moment we've all been anticipating: getting the heck out of dodge. As I mentioned in the previous chapter, this is the romanticized image that a lot of aspiring preppers have: the man, complete with his perfectly-packed bug out bag attached to his back, leading his family to the mountains beyond to begin their new life, as the remnants of their previous life lay smoldering in the background. In reality, it's not quite that easy. Think about it; if you knew you had 30 minutes to assemble what you needed to evacuate your home for good, what all would you pack? Have you ever sat down and considered it? The impact of leaving home and striking out into the unknown will not only affect you, but your family as well.

The concept of leaving everything you know and venturing out into the unknown with your family should not be something that is taken lightly. For the sake of our discussion here, we will discuss similar scenarios to the ones brought up in the previous chapter about bugging in. It should quickly become apparent that this is a measure of last resort.

Let's consider another weather-related scenario. Suppose you live in an area that is in the midst of record-shattering rainfall. Everywhere you look, the floodwaters continue their march towards your home, with no end in sight for the rain. You've already set out all the sandbags you could muster up on short notice, but they are simply not enough. The time has come to make a choice, and it seems that bugging out is the logical decision. Once you've secured your residence to the best of your ability, how do you go about leaving?

Simply put, there are two options to choose from when it comes to bugging out: by vehicle or by foot. Regardless of which method you choose, you are going to want to have some basic supplies with you. I would recommend you (and your spouse) have the same basic loadout and your kids, if old enough, also have bug out bags that are suited to their age and size. This way, each family member can carry some of the burden, rather than having one huge duffle bag that weighs you down after 50 feet. The ideal bug out bag for you and your spouse would stay in the 25 to 35 pound range. While that may sound extremely light considering all you will want to cram into it, the reality of it is, anything more than that is going to simply create hardship down the road as your pack will become more of a hindrance than a help. And let's remember, the purpose of this bag is to keep you and your family safe for up to 72 hours. It's not going to provide creature comforts. When it comes to young children, I would keep their packs around 10 pounds if possible, with weight increasing the older they are. This is likely going to limit them to the basics such as food and water, flashlight, and a change of socks and underwear.

As far as contents of your bug out bag go, this is another one of those areas where if you ask 10 different people, you will get 10 different answers. For our purposes, I will provide a list of the absolute bare essentials. As I have stated before, your circumstances will likely vary and it will be up to you to decide if there are items that you need to add to your load out. I would just caution you to have each member of your family try out their bags on a short hike, just so everyone knows what it will feel like to carry their supplies. This will let you know, rather quickly, if there is too much weight present or if you have the flexibility to add more gear. Again, the time to acquaint yourself with your bug out bag is not the moment that you set foot out the door to evacuate.

In regards to contents, here are my personal thoughts. Some of it mirrors the FEMA recommendations for what you need to keep on hand in your home emergency kit. Feel free to add or replace items depending on your specific circumstances, and you will find a checklist in the back of the book that you can use to set up your bag and catalog what you deem necessary to keep in it should you be forced to evacuate on foot. When selecting a bag, try out several different types to see which works best for you. Surplus military ALICE packs are very popular and reasonably priced. Others prefer standard internal or external frame hiking backpacks. Still others prefer the more tactical type bag with external webbing and scores of individual pockets. Only you can decide what works best for your specific situation. There will be some redundancies between you and your spouse's bag, as well as your children's. This allows you to still have the necessary gear should one bag be lost, etc.

Adult Bug Out Bag

Water – There are several options to carrying water in your bugout bag. Hydration bladders are a very popular way of carrying a large amount of water in a small amount of space. Other methods are reusable water bottles, such as the Nalgene line of bottles, and the Datrex brand water pouches. Whichever method you choose, it would be wise to consider an additional method of sterilizing water when, or if, you consume your immediate supply. This could be in the form of a water purifying filter, such as the offerings from Sawyer, Lifestraw, and SteriPEN, or as simple as iodine tablets. You would also do well to consider a method of storing larger amounts of water for cooking, sanitation, etc. Several companies make collapsible water carriers that weigh next to nothing while empty. The 3 day rule still applies, but since weight is of an issue, we are not taking sanitation into account in our estimates. The average human needs around a half gallon of water per day to stay healthy. Since water is around 8 pounds per gallon, it's easy to see how this will be one of the major components of your bug out bag, so plan accordingly.

Food — Once again, the 3 day rule applies here. Fortunately, dehydrated food takes up little space and requires only water, at the most, to prepare. Many companies sell pre-made 72 hour kits of dehydrated, 25 year shelf life emergency food that fit perfectly into a bug out bag. However, if you like, you can customize your loadout. Some people prefer canned or pre-packaged meats such as spam, Vienna sausages, tuna, etc. There's also the camper's staple of ramen noodles. Protein, granola, and cereal bars are popular, as well as peanuts, pop tarts, and beef jerky. Foods that are ready-to-eat out of the package are certainly advantageous, such as military MRE's (meals, ready to eat). Be aware, though, that MRE's can be quite heavy and cumbersome, and some require a form of heat for the I. Remember to be cognizant of where your bag will be stored and of the expiration dates of your contents. No one wants to be eating tuna that's 12 months expired, even during an emergency situation. I personally have a few of the emergency food ration bars in my vehicle bag that are sold through various prepper outlets. They keep for up to 5 years, are relatively inexpensive, and can be broken apart to ration out. They take up little space, so you can easily pack 3 days' worth in your pack. You may have to experiment to see what works for not only your needs, but your family's as well.

Finally, a good, lightweight container to boil water in would be advisable to pack. It can aid in the preparation of dehydrated foods as well as preparing coffee, tea, etc. There are small mess kits available that fold into themselves and take up little room and weight. A small bag of plastic utensils would be a great addition as well.

Shelter – This area can be as complex or as simple as you care to make it. A tent is the obvious choice when it comes to portable shelter. However, most weigh upwards of 15 pounds and can be bulky to carry. There are companies that make tents that weigh in the single digits that take up very little space. The downfall is that most of them cost several hundred dollars or more. If that's within your budget, one tent each in you and your spouse's bag would provide the perfect shelter for a family. If that is simply not in your budget, you might consider a quality tarp. There are some available with built-in tie downs to secure it between trees to provide a covered area to camp in. They won't keep out the bugs, but it will keep you out of the rain and wind, especially when suspended on a single line between two trees and the sides secured to the ground. One thing that you should consider if you choose a tarp is some method of lashing it to your pack. Since a large tarp will provide coverage, yet take up precious room inside your bag, it may be more advisable to roll it up, like one does a sleeping bag, and lash it to the bottom of your bag. This is somewhere that paracord may come in quite handy, since it will have a myriad of other uses in addition to securing your tarp.

When it comes to sleeping, a traditional sleeping bag would be nice, but for most preppers, it's simply too large and cumbersome. Some companies, such as SOL, sell an emergency bivvy sack that are extremely lightweight, yet retain lots of heat. There are also the old standby "space blankets" which can work in a pinch as well.

If getting off the ground is a priority, there are several companies that make survival hammocks that weigh merely a few pounds and are available in models with mosquito netting and a rain fly built in. As with food and water, your options are many, so do your research and choose wisely. Remember that you can mix and match products with your spouse if necessary in order to ensure that you have the most optimal emergency setup. Just remember to keep the weights of your bags in line with the person carrying it.

Clothing – It should be quite obvious that the space limitations of the bug out bag will make packing more than the basic clothing requirements prohibitive. Since we are talking about (hopefully) a short term situation, your true needs should be quite minimal: a long sleeve shirt, long pants, a change of underwear, and a spare pair of socks. While some might advocate shorts and short sleeve shirts during the warmer months, protection from the sun, insects, and vegetation associated with being in the wilderness make it very advisable that skin be covered. Your choice of shoes should be that of a sturdy variety that provides support for both your foot and ankle. This is an area that you need to update seasonally. During the warmer months, a lighter, quick-drying fabric will be advisable for the shirt and pants and vice versa during the colder months. In an emergency situation, wardrobe changes will be infrequent at best, so go ahead and mentally prepare yourself for that possibility, as unpleasant as it may seem to you or other members of your family.

A few extras, space permitting, that are recommended would be a head covering, such as a hat or toboggan, gloves, and a lightweight poncho. All of the clothing should be stored in a waterproof bag and can be further condensed by using one of the vacuum bag storage systems, therefore taking up less of your valuable space.

Fire starting and lighting – Both you and your spouse should carry some form of fire starting device and a method of illumination. This is another category where the sky is the limit. Some people prefer a waterproof bag full of disposable lighters, whereas others prefer boxes of matches. There are also several quality fire starters on the market that produce a hot spark when scraped. Pre-made fire starter cubes make it easier to get a campfire going, especially when dry wood is hard to find.

When it comes to lighting, there are many options available. The headlamp is a popular choice because it is both lightweight and hands-free. A good, compact, high-lumen flashlight or lightweight, collapsible lantern is a good choice as well. Regardless of your choice, I would ensure that all take the same size battery in order to minimize the number of spares that you need to have packed as well.

Communication – While you will likely have your cell phone with you, it's wise to have a backup form of communication with your family, should you get separated or you are traveling with a group. At a minimum, I would try to have a backup cell phone charger that is solar powered. Standard two-way radios have limited range, but for most circumstances, would likely suffice. A better option would be a handheld HAM radio. They send and receive just like a standard two-way, yet they have the added capability of both UHF and VHF and offer extended range. A radio that I see often recommended is the Baofeng UV-5RA. They are affordable, coming in at around $40 or less, and have all the features that a beginning HAM operator would need. With this type of device, some training and education beforehand will be required, but it is relatively simple to become proficient with.

If space permits, you may also want to consider an emergency radio that has multiple power options such as battery, solar, and hand crank. There are many styles available from manufacturers such as Eton, Midland, Kaito, and Grundig. Many of these will be able to pick up AM and FM stations, as well as have NOAA weather capability. A radio can provide a sense of comfort, since you will have the availability of hearing news about whatever situation you are facing, as well as being able to stay ahead of whatever weather may be heading your way. In addition, some of the hand crank radios offer cell phone charging capability, keeping that smart phone up and running, even if it's just for your kids to play games on. Keeping spirits up, especially among little ones, will be extremely beneficial during an emergency.

Tools – When it comes to tools that I would carry in my bug out bag, I would try and keep it to three items. The first one would be a quality multi-tool such as the classic Leatherman tool or the traditional Swiss Army Knife. In addition to a standard cutting blade, there are numerous other implements that can come in quite handy while in the great outdoors.

My second choice would be a quality folding pocket knife. My daily carry is a Benchmade Griptilian. It's around 6 inches long, maintains a great edge, locks up tighter than a bank vault, and has a great pocket clip. Mine's seen its share of abuse, but it keeps on ticking. It retails for around $100. If that's not in your budget, there are several manufacturers that offer quality knives for a lower price. Check out Buck, Kershaw, Case, Gerber, etc. This is an area where a little research can pay off in droves, so do your due diligence when selecting this item.

The third item I would pack would be a good fixed blade sheath knife or a small hatchet. The purpose of this tool would be to chop kindling and perform other tasks around camp or on the trail. The hatchet is more suited to this role, but can be heavier, so take that into consideration. A good fixed blade knife with a solid tang (where the blade is one long piece of steel with the handles installed around it) will do just as good in the hands of a competent user. Again, buyer beware on these, as you don't want your $25 piece of Chinese steel breaking off right in the middle of trying to split kindling. I would look into the Geber, Kabar, and ESEE brands of knives as a good place to start.

First Aid – While you can make your own kit, this is one area that a pre-packaged kit can come in handy. Companies such as Adventure Medical Kits make a variety of models to suit the size of your group and the level of care you wish to provide. They come in fold out pouches that keep the gear organized and sometimes have room for you to add a few of your own items. I would have some sort of kit in each family members' bag. Additionally, a blood stop kit, such as those from Quik Clot, would help treat a larger wound. If you are cheap like me, you also have tampons and maxi pads in your first aid gear already. They are great for puncture wounds and take up little room in your first aid gear.

Hygiene – In keeping with our minimalist weight goals, one has to be selective in what all the pack in this department. Some toothpaste, a toothbrush, flossers, small rolls of toilet paper, and hand sanitizer would fit the bill. You could also pack a bar of soap, but some prefer unscented baby wipes in order to quickly clean off the grime from the previous day. Small, compressed wash towels are available as well that expand to the size of a standard wash cloth when opened and wetted. Other companies offer various combination shampoo / soaps that can be used to get the sweat and dirt off. You can look at the various options and decide what works best for you.

You will also want to ensure that your spouse's pack has a supply of feminine hygiene products on board as well. As stated in the first aid section, the tampons and maxi pads can serve double roles as first aid items if needed.

Self Defense – This is one of those areas that you will have to decide what's best for you and your family. If you are heading to a secluded area where you will not likely encounter other evacuees, you may forego this category. If you see that you will likely encounter other groups, you may want to consider some form of defense, be it a firearm or a less lethal option. Again, training and knowledge of the law will play a role here, depending on what you choose. Be advised that if you are bugging out to a government evacuee center, most types of weapons will not be allowed on the premises.

If one is going the route of packing a handgun, a good compromise, if encounters with people are unlikely, would be a 22 caliber handgun. These can be found in lightweight models and one can carry extra magazines or a box or two of ammunition for very little space and weight. A handgun such as this could be useful for small game hunting if the event is protracted and additional food is needed. It can also be pressed into service if signaling for rescue is needed.

Just remember, if you are bugging out, others around you or throughout your immediate area likely are as well. Take care to not draw undue attention to yourself and your family. I know a lot of experts in the prepper field will discourage the use of "tactical" appearing backpacks with the explanation that if a nervous or desperate evacuee spots you with your tactical-looking pack, you will more likely be targeted for harassment or attack. While I can see the merit to the argument, I would personally put that concern at the back of the list. In a bug out situation, most people will likely be carrying what they can in whatever they can. Whether it be a tactical OD backpack with MOLLE webbing or a Kelty external frame hiking pack, the appearance of being prepared will single you out regardless.

 In a situation such as this, I would advocate staying away from groups of people if at all possible. In the absence of rule of law, it's just you against the world. When your family is at risk, consider any alternative that would allow you to avoid crowds. Sometimes avoidance of a situation is the best defense.

Other – To finish up our well-packed bug out bag, I would personally add a few last items. First would be a roll of quality duct tape. The old adage about duct tape being able to fix anything may not be completely right, but it sure will help out in the majority of situations where a quick fix may be required. It can be used to cover tears in the fabric of your pack, aid in building a shelter, and even be pressed into service for first aid if necessary.

I would also have a small amount of paracord for lashing items to your pack, among many other uses. It's lightweight and won't take up much room, and if needed, can be separated into individual strands as well.

As in our home kit, I would have some cash on hand since no electronic devices will be operating if the grid is down in the immediate area. Maybe a few hundred dollars in bills no larger than a twenty. Personal identification would be a good idea as well.

Spare batteries and bulbs for your radios, flashlights, etc. are a must. It would be wise to have devices consolidated to one battery size, minimizing the number of spare batteries necessary to pack.

I would definitely pack some sort of maps of the local area. Topographical maps are great, provided you know how to read them. A standard road atlas would be beneficial as well. I would make sure to have a few destinations selected beforehand. Nothing is more dangerous or risky than simply striking out on foot. Know how to reach friends and family by means other than the main roads. Perhaps a walk up and down a ridge will be shorter than following the highway. Maybe your destination is your hunting camp or favorite fishing spot. Just be aware that any public camping or recreational areas will likely be flooded with people who had the exact same idea. A secluded place is your best bet if you are in a situation where law and order is suspended. Since you will likely be spending a good amount of time outdoors, I would add in some form of sunscreen and bug repellent as well.

If law and order are present, it might be a good idea to consider local government buildings and places of worship, as these locations will likely be transformed into community shelters in the event of a massive emergency. While most of us have GPS capability on our smart phones, we simply cannot rely on this during a grid-down situation where service may be spotty or non-existent. Knowing where you are going and how to covertly get there will eliminate a lot of the threat of being caught in a crowd of panicked people and will hopefully keep you and your family out of harm's way. Emergencies bring out the worst in some people, and you can never underestimate what a desperate person may be capable of. Plan your bug out destination well in advance; it will pay off in more ways than you can count.

I would also pack a few large, black garbage bags. These can be used for a variety of purposes: bag cover, sanitation, water collection, etc.

Finally, I would pack some moleskin, or some other form of blister treatment, in the first aid kit. Blisters and raw skin will likely begin to form after a short time if one's shoes aren't fully broken in or the terrain is very rugged and demanding. This material will minimize the intensity of the situation, hopefully keeping everyone relatively mobile.

As in every situation that we have discussed, you may need to alter the contents of your bug out bag to fit your individual situation. This is not an area to get hasty in. Sit down, make a list, discuss it as a family, and truly consider what's necessary and what is not. In a survival scenario, you aren't looking for all the comforts of home and a bag that could carry everything including the kitchen sink. You are looking at carrying only the necessary supplies to keep you and your family safe until the timing is right to return home or you reach your destination.

Children's Bug Out Bag

The amount of gear that your child or children can carry will obviously be dictated by their age and physical limitations. However, as with the adult bags, there are a few basic supplies that should be carried. Anything beyond the basics is subject to what they are capable of safely carrying. Since fear and hesitancy will likely be running rampant through their minds, you should remember to not exacerbate the situation by overloading them with gear that they simply cannot carry.

Water – Once again, the three days rule applies here. All but the smallest children should be able to carry a three day supply of water in their pack.

Food – While you could duplicate the dehydrated food loadout that is in the adult bags, it may be more prudent to go with the lightweight offerings such as pop tarts, ramen noodles, protein / granola bars, etc. If nothing else, having a variety of food divided amongst your family will help break up any monotony of eating the same food for several meals in a row.

Clothing – Spare socks, underwear, and long shirt and pants, sealed up in a waterproof bag.

Other – Since we are keeping weight to an absolute minimum, I would only add a few additional items to any young child's bag. The first would be a lightweight headlamp or small flashlight. For the most lightweight illumination, you may look into the military snap lights. They come in a variety of colors, last several hours, and require no batteries. The second would be a coloring book, drawing pad, stuffed animal, etc. from home that can serve as both a comfort item to the child and be used to pass the time. Finally, I would include a small first aid kit that has the bare essentials such as bandages, gauze pads, and anti-septic cream.

It may be a struggle to keep the bag lightweight enough for a young child to carry, but as they grow, they can begin to shoulder more of their own gear. This will allow you to not only let them carry their own sleeping shelter, etc., it will allow more flexibility in what all the family as a whole can pack.

One must also take into consideration the difficulties of bugging out with an infant or newborn. This situation drastically changes everything, as the bug out bag requirements will rise exponentially with the requirements of a young child. This is the worst possible scenario in which to bug out. If this is the situation that you find yourself in, truly do your homework in advance, plotting the quickest overland routes to a destination that has the help and resources you will need to care for your young child. I pray that none of you ever find yourselves in this position, but advance planning here may literally mean the difference between life and death.

Once your bug out bags are complete, each member of the family should go for a long walk while wearing them. It need not be a strenuous affair through the mountains, as the purpose is to ensure that the bags are not overburdened for each family member and that they are all properly adjusted and fitted to each member. Again, a little time spent during a non-emergency getting your gear fitted will pay off in droves should you ever need to press it into service for the real thing.

Now that we have discussed the concept and realities of what all is involved in bugging out by foot, let's consider the other bug out method mentioned at the beginning of the chapter: the vehicle.

Imagine that your city is on the verge of a major court decision, as referenced to earlier. Tensions run high, and there is a heavy police presence to deter the chaos that so easily results in these situations. If you find yourself in this scenario, it would be wise to consider your options. If all heck breaks loose, how quickly can you be loaded up in the family bug out vehicle and on the road? Once the violence is at a fever pitch, the trouble makers may be going door to door or house to house bringing mayhem and destruction. You have to decide when the appropriate is time to get out of Dodge.

Just as you would monitor an approaching storm, monitor the social situation with as much diligence. Since you won't be carrying everything on your back, it's much easier to preposition everything in your vehicle, along with any extra items that you would like to carry with you. Now is the time to fill the gas tank with your extra gas if it's not already sitting on full. If your gut tells you that it's time to leave, trust it. Secure your residence the best you can, load up your family and bug out bags, and get out of the area. For us men, the thought of leaving the homestead to potential destruction from Mother Nature or the wrath of angry protesters doesn't sit well. Our home is our castle and we aren't keen on leaving it vulnerable.

However, this is one of those situations where you cannot let emotion override your common sense. If the situation is bad enough that violence is spreading faster than the authorities can quell it, then it's time to go. I would urge you not to wait until it's banging on your front door. As difficult as it may be, load your family up and bug out to your nearest safe destination that you have planned in advance. Hopefully, the unrest will subside, and you can return home in a short period. If not, then you have your bug out bags and anything else you packed in your vehicle to get you by until it does. Your possessions can be replaced. That's why we all have, or should have, insurance. Don't let your pride get in the way of protecting your family. An AR15 and a hundred loaded mags may be the Hollywood version of making a stand, but in reality, taking on an angry mob rarely works out in one's favor. Better to bug out and live to fight another day.

It should be clear by now that the concept of bugging out should be reserved only for the most severe of situations. It is not to be taken lightly, especially if conditions dictate that it be done by foot. However, if you have thoroughly examined the scenario and conclude that this is, in fact, your only option, then DO NOT HESITATE. Waiting too long may result in increased risk and danger to your family.

Chapter 9

Communication

We live in an era that most everyone, including young children, owns a smart phone of some make and model. I would wager to say a large percentage of the population, if asked, would say that they couldn't function without their device. Most of us guys are guilty as well, as we use our phones or tablets to escape while our wives are watching some show that we just can't stomach. What would we do if, all of a sudden, all the signals went down and our phones were reduced to nothing more than expensive paperweights?

Apocalyptic scenarios of nationwide EMP's and solar storms aside, the possibility of losing cell phone service is quite probable in an area experiencing a major storm system as cell towers may be adversely affected. In addition, in this age of "lone wolf" terror attacks, who's to say that a power plant or cell phone network won't be targeted for destruction? For these reasons alone, it's important to have a plan in place prior to something like this occurring.

Every family needs to have a plan in place where they meet up in the event of an emergency. As we've discussed in prior chapters, having multiple escape destinations planned out well in advance is one of the cornerstones of having a viable emergency plan. However, what do you do if something occurs while the family is split up?

Imagine that a terrorist attack takes out your local power company's main substation, plunging most of your city into the dark. If you've prepared an emergency plan, everyone will be able to communicate via phone call or text message and will report home, if safe to do so, or report to the nearest agreed-upon rally site. If the cell phone network is down or jammed with people trying to communicate with friends and loved ones, it would be best to have an action plan agreed upon that everyone follows.

Obviously, your home should be your number one rally point. You and your spouse return home after picking up the children (assuming they are in school, daycare, etc.) and decide then what your next move is. Should your home be compromised, then everyone defaults to the next rally point designated on your list. This could be a relative or family friend in close proximity or even a church or other familiar location. Since you are planning for events that are both weather and man-made in nature, it's best to have multiple areas planned out and agreed upon. If there is someone who picks up your kids, they need to be informed of your action plan as well.

What I would recommend is that you come up with a list of rally points and visit every one of them so that your family is familiar with them. After that, print up directions to these locations from home, school, work, etc. so that each family member knows how to get there both by foot and by vehicle. Then put a copy of this in each child's school backpack and keep one in you and your spouse's wallets. Give additional copies to any caretakers that may help out with your kids. Along with directions and destinations, these lists should also include the phone number and name of the contact at that location.

Since all but a major emergency event will leave the cell network functioning, text and phone calls are still the best method of communication for your family. Still, a plan of action should be in place should that network go down. If all of you live, work, and go to school in close proximity, a network of two-way radios may be a wonderful addition to any laptop bag, backpack, or purse. Models vary in range from less than two miles to more than 10, so research what model will work best. If you are spread over a wider area, consider the portable, handheld HAM radio, such as the Baofeng that I referenced in the previous chapter. It may seem excessive to have this extra item with you at all times, but should the cell network be compromised, it will be worth its weight in gold.

As with all disaster planning, preventative action is where success is made or lost. It does no good to have all the gear without all the understanding. Your whole family needs to be aware of the plans and should any locations or contacts change over time, the rally point information should be updated as soon as possible.

Chapter 10

Pets

Now that you are hopefully getting an idea of the proper items to have on hand for an emergency, we need to spend a little time on an area that could be very easily overlooked: our pets.

If you're like me, your animals are part of your family. We have two beagles, an eternally-disgruntled old cat, a hamster, and three aquarium's worth of freshwater fish. What happens if we have to bug in or bug out?

Well, hopefully most of us will never have to face a situation where we have to flee our primary residences. However, even if we do get to shelter in place, we need to have a contingency plan for Rover and any other pets that call our house a home. For dogs and cats, the preparations are probably fairly straight forward. I buy a 20 lb. bag of cat food every three months or so and keep it in a bucket in my garage where the cat spends 90% of her time. This keeps her fed for up to 3 months at a time. Whenever the bucket gets down to about 1/3 full, I buy up another bag. This way, I still have upwards of two weeks' worth of emergency food should we be forced to shelter in place. Water will not be an issue, as we have plenty on hand and she does not consume enough to make a sizeable dent in my stocks.

The same goes for our dogs. Yes, we are the dog owners who give our dogs the fancy dehydrated food that looks like oatmeal once prepared. It comes in a 20 lb. bag that is delivered monthly. I also try to keep a two week reserve of either canned or dry food stocked back for them as well. It need not be expensive, so whatever is on sale is what I get. We periodically mix it in or feed it exclusively to the dogs so that it does not get past its expiration date. As with the cat, the dogs don't consume enough water for it to be an issue. If push comes to shove, we can collect rain water for the animals.

As you can imagine, the dwarf hamster that resides in my daughter's room next to her beta fish does not consume all that much. We keep a large bag of hamster food on hand and replace whenever it gets to about 1/3 full. Buddy the hamster will eat like a king for quite some time even if the grid goes down for a while.

When it comes to fish, this is a little more difficult. My son's three aquariums are filled with fish who eat the frozen, cube-style mixture of shrimp and other nutrients. We try and keep a month supply of it on hand at all times as well. If necessary, we have a large supply of flake food that they can eat as well.

The good news is, unless you have a pack of Great Danes or are the crazy cat lady that you see on the news, keeping extra food for your animals should not be a very big issue. Simply keep the extra food near their normal food and replace as necessary. Since even a 20 lb. bag of food takes up a minimal storage footprint, I would keep as much as necessary on hand to keep your animals fed for up to a month during an emergency.

The tough calls really come when you are faced with having to bug out. This is an area that your own judgement will have to determine your course forward. If leaving by vehicle, it's easy enough to crate your dogs or cats and take them with you to your bug out destination. Be cautious, though, if heading to an evacuee center, as not all of them will allow pets. Plan ahead accordingly so that your family and furry friends are adequately accommodated.

When it comes to animals that you can't evacuate with you, or you are having to bug out on foot, you have to make the best decision you are able to and then move forward with your plan. In our case, we can fill the hamster's bowl with enough food to last a good long while, along with topping off his water bottle. The situation is similar with our cat. I would pour as much dry food as possible along with a large container of water and keep her in the garage and out of the elements.

The dogs would come with us, as they could be leashed and crated with ease, if evacuating by car, or could accompany us on foot if that is the method we are forced to evacuate by.

When it comes to my son's fish, there are feeders available that slowly break down over time. They are designed for situations where the owners may be out of town for some time, therefore providing a time-release source of food. In situations like this, you simply do the best you can and pray that the situation is resolved quickly and you can return home.

If you are forced to evacuate with your pets, you need to consider their needs as well. When it comes to their food and water, you can choose to carry it in your bug out bags, or you can let them carry their own. Many companies make saddlebag-style packs for dogs of various sizes which allow them to carry their own food, water, and vaccination info. Additionally, most dogs and cats can drink from pond or creek water with no ill effects. While dogs are the most likely animals to be seen with evacuees, I know people that would refuse to leave their cats behind. This, again, is where you have to be creative. Perhaps you could put your cat in its crate and pull it in a wagon, or take turns carrying it. There are various methods of transporting animals, so do your due diligence in planning for the four-legged members of your family as well.

One side benefit if evacuating on foot with dogs (especially large breed dogs) is the intimidation factor. While my beagles may not exactly instill fear in someone intending to do me harm, I doubt that my neighbor's German Shephard would elicit the same response. Dogs can also serve as an early warning system against other animals if you are camping in a remote area after bugging out.

Chapter 11

Future Planning

Hopefully by this point, you realize that there is quite a bit to this whole prepping thing. The good news is, you don't have to do it all at once. Start slow, with the bare essentials, and build from there. I have a series of resources and checklists at the end of the book to guide you along in your planning.

Once the basics are covered and your bug out bags are packed, you may very well have been bitten by the prepper bug. You may now see the value in foresightedness and how it will set you apart from your apathetic neighbors. So, where do you go from here?

The answer to that question can only be determined by your individual needs and interests. However, there are several areas that the devoted prepper should have at least a basic knowledge of. These areas can include primitive living techniques, small gardening basics, hunting and trapping, bush-craft, shelter-making, tracking, wilderness medicine, and the basics of mechanics. The skills that were essential to our grandparents and great-grandparents may be just as essential to us someday. How ironic would it be to see the shift in what society deems an "essential" job? Our modern society depends on armies of technicians and engineers to keep our networks up and the grid going. Suppose all that is taken away. All of a sudden, it's the gardener and farmer who is in great demand. The Les Strouds of the world will be in high demand, while the lawyers, network developers, fashion moguls, etc. may be barely scratching out an existence.

If you truly are interested in longer-term planning, I would suggest joining with like-minded individuals. Start a community garden. Add rain barrels to your gutters to harness nature's free water. If your living arrangements allow it, consider raising chickens or other farm animals and learn the complexities of keeping livestock for food and trade. Perhaps you could purchase an older vehicle and restore it, learning everything about it as you go about your work. Anything that makes you reliant on yourself rather than others for your day-to-day existence will be of benefit.

There are several places to increase your knowledge of this subject. In my town, we have a prepper store called P5 Preparedness (a link is in the back of the book) and the staff there are ready and willing to help you take your first step into prepping or can help the experienced prepper further refine their planning. Weekly discussion groups delve into the various facets of prepping and can be greatly beneficial.

Online forums and printed publications can be helpful as well. Just make sure that the information fits with your situation and that it is legitimate and practical. There are lots of people out there spouting all kinds of advice who have probably never set foot in the woods. Develop relationships with people or groups who can not only talk the talk, but can walk the walk as well.

In closing, I hope that this book has been helpful to the man who may have never given a second thought to the concept of preparedness. To reiterate my point from the opening of the book, men are the foundations of their families. It's tasked to us to be the providers of not only monetary security, but physical and emotional security as well. In my opinion, this world is full of far too many men who obsess only about themselves. To be honest, that's a shameful thing. If you have finished this book and a flame has been lit, then I've done my job. The rest is up to you. As I've stated before, preparedness is not simply buying and packing up a bunch of gear. It's the knowledge behind why you bought it and how you'll use it to help your family weather the storms of life that's the real key to it all. I sincerely hope that you and your family never have to use the information contained in these pages. But should the need arise, I hope I have given you both a checklist and a mindset that will allow you to get through an emergency situation and emerge better from it.

This world seems to get very dark at times, and it would be easy to just throw up one's hands in surrender. Real men don't do that. Real men examine the information I've given here and then examine their own lives. If you come to the conclusion that I did, you realize that there are a lot of things that simply don't matter in the long run. Men, take care of your families. Not just now, but plan for down the road as well. We never know what Mother Nature or the minds of evil men may throw at us, but with a little bit of forethought, a lot of the chaos and fear can be avoided, or at least minimized.

I hope that the concept of prepping opens up new adventures for your families. I know when my family goes hiking in the mountains near our home, my kids will point out places and say that we could camp there, or plant a garden there, etc. Turn prepping into an activity that is not viewed as work, but as fun. Take your spouse or oldest child out one weekend with nothing but the contents of your bug out bag and vow to last 48 hours in the wilderness. Exercises like this will not only expose weaknesses in your plan, but they will help form a bond between husband and wife or father and child that may not have been as strong as it now is. Involve your kids in it to the best degree possible. Point out what types of fish are the best to eat while fishing from the creek bank. Teach your kids which tracks belong to which animals. Maybe plant a small vegetable garden out back to grow the vegetables you most often eat. Small steps will lead to big results. Some emergency food companies have monthly plans available to stock up over time. Take it one step at a time, and you can be better prepared to handle life-changing events than you ever thought possible. It's a journey. Are you ready to get started?

Chapter 12

Resources

Below you will find a series of resources that will help you not only gather the items needed to assemble your bug out bags, etc., but will point you towards information that will help you grow and expand your knowledge of the concept of preparedness and all that it encompasses. Bear in mind that this is just a small representation of the products and information available to the beginning prepper. I merely wanted to give a sampling of products available to beginning preppers of all budgets. In addition to the info below, there are several prepper-themed apps available for smart phones that help organize and categorize your gear and planning.

Home Resources:

Generators:

Generac:

http://www.generac.com/

Kohler :

http ://www.kohlergenerators.com/index.html

Honda :

http ://m.powerequipment.honda.com/generators

Northern Tools:

http://m.northerntool.com/categories/shop~tools~category_generators?hotline=false

Harbor Freight:

http://m.harborfreight.com/catalogsearch/result?q=Generator

Storm Shelters / Safe Rooms:

Fain Storm Shelters:

http://fainstormshelters.com/

Family Safe Shelters:

http://familysafeshelters.com/

Tornado Alley Armor:

http://www.tornadoalleyarmor.com/

Ground Zero Storm Shelters:

http://www.groundzeroshelters.com/flattop.html

Bug Out Bags / Backpacks:

LA Police Gear:

http://www.lapolicegear.com/bags-and-packs.html

Condor:

http://tacticalgear.com/condor-bags-and-packs

LL Bean:

http://m.llbean.com/productlist.html?nav=main&bc=97&skCatId=916#916

Maxpedition:

http://www.maxpedition.com/store/pc/Bags-Packs-c2.htm

Kelty:

https://kelty.com/backpacks/

North Face:

https://www.thenorthface.com/shop/equipment-backpacks

Eberlestock:

https://www.eberlestock.com/Packs.htm

Blackhawk:

http://www.blackhawk.com/Products/Tactical-Nylon/Bags-Packs/Bags.aspx

Surplus military ALICE packs:

https://www.armysurplusworld.com/category/packs?cat=1885

Navigation:

Rand McNally Maps:

http://www.randmcnally.com/product/road-atlas

Topozone Topographical maps:

http://www.topozone.com/

Knives:

Smokey Mountain Knife Works:

https://www.smkw.com/

Buck Knives:

http://www.buckknives.com/

Case Knives:

http://www.wrcase.com/index_en.php

Kabar Knives:

https://www.kabar.com/

SOG Knives:

https://www.sogknives.com/

ESEE Knives:

http://www.eseeknives.com/

Benchmade Knives:

http://www.benchmade.com/

Victorinox Swiss Army Knives:

https://www.victorinox.com/us/en

Leatherman Multi-tools:

http://www.leatherman.com/

Gerber Knives and Multi-tools:

http://www.gerbergear.com/

Communication / Emergency / Weather Radios:

Oregon Scientific:

http://store.oregonscientific.com/us/

Midland:

https://midlandusa.com/

Cobra:

http://www.cobra.com/products/walkie-talkies-two-way-radios

Baofeng:

http://www.baofengradio.com/en/ProShowcn.asp?ID=141

Eton:

http://www.etoncorp.com/en

Grundig:

https://www.amazon.com/Grundig-S450DLX-Deluxe-Shortwave-Radio/dp/B004FV4ND0

Kaito:

http://www.kaitousa.com/

Solar Cell Phone Chargers:

http://www.toptenreviews.com/mobile/accessories/best-solar-phone-chargers/

Self Defense (Lethal / Non-lethal):

Bud's Gun Shop (Lethal):

https://www.budsgunshop.com/catalog/mobile/

GT Distributors (Lethal / Non-lethal) :

https://www.gtdist.com/

Survival Sullivan Blog (Non-lethal weapons article):

http://www.survivalsullivan.com/non-lethal-self-defense-weapons-for-edc/

Automotive Fuel Storage:

Standard 5 Gallon Plastic Gas Cans:

http://m.harborfreight.com/5-gallon-gas-can-67997.html?utm_referrer=direct%2Fnot%20provided

NATO Jerry Cans:

http://www.lexingtoncontainercompany.com/Nato-Jerry-Cans.html

Stabil Fuel Stabilizers :

https ://www.goldeagle.com/product/sta-bil-fuel-stabilizer

Automotive Emergency Gear:

Battery Booster / Air Compressors:

http://m.harborfreight.com/4-in-1-jump-starter-with-air-compressor-62374.html?utm_referrer=direct%2Fnot%20provided

Flat Tire Fixes:

http://www.fixaflat.com/us/index.php

Tow Straps / Tow Ropes:

http://www.4wheelparts.com/Winches-Winch-Accessories/Tow-Strap.aspx?t_c=18&t_s=190&t_pt=5083

Road Flares:

http://www.orionsignals.com/application/highway.html

Medical / First Aid Supplies:

Adventure Medical:

http://www.adventuremedicalkits.com/

Zee Medical:

http://www.zeemedical.com/us/first-aid-supplies/first-aid-kit

Grainger Industrial Supply:

https://m.grainger.com/mobile/category/first-aid-kits/first-aid-and-wound-care/safety/ecatalog/N-oau?redirect=first+aid+kits&suggestConfigId=6&searchRedirect=first+aid+kits&searchBar=true

Quik Clot Products:

http://www.quikclot.com/

E-firstaidsupplies:

http://www.e-firstaidsupplies.com/

Flashlights, Lanterns, etc:

Surefire:

http://www.surefire.com/illumination/flashlights.html

Petzl:

https://m.petzl.com/US/en/Sport/Lighting

Streamlight:

http://m.streamlight.com/en-us

Coleman:

http://www.coleman.com/coleman-lighting-batterylanterns/

Maglite:

http://maglite.com/

Emergency Food Supplies:

Wise Foods:

http://www.wisefoodstorage.com/

Augason Farms:

https://www.walmart.com/c/brand/augason-farms

Mountain House:

http://www.mountainhouse.com/

Protein Bars :

https ://www.moreprepared.com/emergency-preparedness-supplies/new-millennium-energy-bar-48-pack.html ?gclid=Cj0KEQjw1K2_BRC0s6jtgJzB-aMBEiQA-WzDMTQLqsscLENe9ygACRvL2N7v1RujvXXyCBy8knWErdIaAk7L8P8HAQ

Bar Rations:

https://www.moreprepared.com/emergency-preparedness-supplies/sos-food-lab-2400-calorie-food-bar.html

Food 4 Patriots:

https://secure.food4patriots.com/

Military MRE's:

https://www.thereadystore.com/mre

Mess Kit:

https://www.amazon.com/Stansport-360-Stainless-Steel-Mess/dp/B0000AQO5S

Emergency Water, Storage, Filtration:

Datrex Water Pouches:

http://www.datrex.com/index/catalogdetail/pdt_id/43

Sawyer Water Filters:

https://sawyer.com/products/type/water-filtration/

MSR Water Filters:

http://www.cascadedesigns.com/msr/water/category

Lifestraw Water Filters:

http://lifestraw.com/

SteriPEN Water Filters:

https://www.steripen.com/

Waterbob Storage Bladder:

https://www.waterbob.com/Welcome.do;jsessionid=8FCC175AA4E858CB9C906B4A414FB883

Nalgene Water Bottles:

http://www.nalgene.com/

Emergency Shelter:

Tarps:

http://tarps.com/

http://www.selfrelianceoutfitters.com/tarps-3/

http://offgridsurvival.com/tarpshelter/

Coleman Tents :

http ://www.coleman.com/coleman-tentsandshelters/

Kelty Tents:

https://kelty.com/tents-shelters/

SOL Bivvy Sacks :

https ://www.surviveoutdoorslonger.com/

Hammocks :

http ://www.cleverhiker.com/best-backpacking-hammocks/

Online / Retail Outlets to shop for preparedness gear:

Walmart:

https://www.walmart.com/search/?query=survival&typeahead=survival&cat_id=0

Emergency Essentials:

http://beprepared.com/

Southern Survival:

http://southernsurvivalgear.com/products

P5 Preparedness:

http://www.p5preparedness.com/

TruPrep:

http://truprep.com/

Coghlans:

http://www.coghlans.com/

Sportsman's Guide:

http://www.sportsmansguide.com/productlist/camping/emergency-supplies?d=117&c=166

Cheaper than Dirt:

https://www.cheaperthandirt.net/category/survival-gear.do?gclid=Cj0KEQjw1K2_BRC0s6jtgJzB-aMBEiQA-WzDMe00gbfx1U631EMfHIJ_A291V9-t_1nYLSdc6LXBmHMaAoZu8P8HAQ

Old Grouch's Military Surplus:

http://www.oldgrouch.com/

Coleman:

http://www.coleman.com/

Bass Pro Shops:

http://m.basspro.com/Camping/_/T-12325000000

Cabela's:

http://www.cabelas.com/category/Camping/104795280.uts

Academy Sports:

http://www.academy.com/shop/browse/camping—outdoors

Gander Mountain :

http ://m.gandermountain.com/camping/

__Training / General Info / Classes on Preparedness:__

American Red Cross:

http://www.redcross.org/index.jsp

FEMA:

https://www.fema.gov/

Ready.gov:

https://www.ready.gov/

P5 Preparedness:

http://www.p5preparedness.com/

Emergency Essentials Blog:

http://beprepared.com/blog?HP=SUB-1/

Chapter 13

Checklists

Use the below checklists to aid in establishing your emergency / bug out plans. I have left blank spaces for you to fill in items that are specific to your individual circumstances.

Household Emergency Kit / Supplies

3 day supply of non-perishable food (each person)   _____

3 day supply of water (each person)   _____

Extra water storage (water bob, barrel, etc.)   _____

Tarps   _____

Fire extinguisher (one for each floor of your house)   _____

Emergency radio with NOAA capability   _____

Flashlights / Headlamps / Lanterns   _____

Extra batteries   _____

First aid kit   _____

Signal whistle   _____

Portable cell phone charger   _____

Dust masks / respirators   _____

Plastic sheeting   _____

Moist towelettes / baby wipes   _____

Garbage bags   _____

Tool Kit (including wrench for shutting off gas, water, etc.) _____

Manual can opener (if your emergency food is in cans) _____

Local road / topographical maps _____

Extra prescription medication / glasses _____

Infant needs (if applicable – formula, diapers, etc.) _____

Pet needs (food, water, medication, leashes, crates) _____

Copies / flash drive of important documents _____

Emergency cash _____

Survival / First Aid manuals _____

 Sleeping bags / blankets _____

Change of clothes / shoes for each family member _____

Household bleach with medicine dropper _____

Matches / fire starting device _____

Personal hygiene items _____

5 gallon bucket with lid _____

Disposable plates, cups, utensils _____

Children's Activities _____

Pens / pencils and notepad _____

Generator (optional) _____

Storm Shelter (optional) _____

Emergency vehicle fuel _____

Other _____ _____

Other _____ _____

Automobile Emergency Kit

3 day supply of food   _____

3 day supply of drinking water   _____

Jumper cables   _____

Tool kit (hammer, phillips and regular screwdrivers,

pliers, socket set, hose clamps, zip ties)   _____

First aid kit   _____

Flashlight (with spare batteries)   _____

Road flares   _____

Small fire extinguisher   _____

Blanket   _____

Cell phone charger   _____

Tire gauge   _____

Emergency tire sealant   _____

Gloves   _____

Roll of duct tape / electrical tape   _____

Tow strap / tow rope   _____

Utility tool (Leatherman / Swiss Army knife)   _____

Poncho   _____

Ice scraper   _____

Small folding shovel   _____

Factory spare tire   _____

Factory jack / tire tool   _____

Air compressor / jump starter box (optional)   _____

Bag of cat litter (optional)   _____

Road Atlas   _____

Other _____   _____

Other _____   _____

Other _____   _____

Pet Supplies

Extra Food   _____

Extra Water   _____

Extra Medications (if applicable)   _____

Leashes / collars / crates   _____

Vaccination Info   _____

Other _____   _____

Items to Rotate / Check Expiration Dates

Emergency food supplies (home / auto / bug out bags)   _____

Emergency water supplies (home / auto / bug out bags)   _____

Emergency prescription medication / first aid supplies   _____

Emergency vehicle fuel   _____

Other _____   _____

First Aid Kits (house / auto / bug out bags)

Extra prescription medications   _____

Alcohol pads / antiseptic wash   _____

Peroxide   _____

Assortment of bandages   _____

Assortment of gauze pads   _____

Medical tape   _____

Assortment of sterile dressings   _____

Tweezers   _____

Scissors / EMT shears   _____

Small flashlight   _____

Aspirin / Ibuprofen (child and adult strength)   _____

Burn relief cream / gel   _____

Anti-bacterial crème   _____

Bug bite relief crème   _____

Disposable cold packs   _____

Splint (limb and finger size)   _____

Stomach / heartburn medication   _____

Thermometer   _____

Small surgical kit (scalpel, forceps, etc.)   _____

Quick Clot blood stopper kit   _____

Other _____   _____

Individual Bug-Out Bags

3 day supply of drinking water   _____

Water purification device   _____

Extra capacity water storage / transport method   _____

3 day food supply   _____

Container / mess kit for cooking   _____

Utensils   _____

Shelter (tarp, tent, bivvy sack, space blanket, etc.)   _____

Paracord   _____

Spare clothing (socks, underwear, long pants / shirt) _____

Head cover (hat, toboggan, shemagh, etc.)   _____

Gloves   _____

Poncho   _____

Fire Starting method (flint & striker, lighter, matches, etc.) _____

Illumination method (flashlight, headlamp, lantern, etc.) _____

Communication method (cell phone, 2 way radio, etc.) _____

Emergency Radio with NOAA capability   _____

Multi tool (Leatherman, Swiss Army Knife, etc.)   _____

Quality folding knife   _____

Quality fixed blade knife or hatchet   _____

First Aid kit (with blood stopper, moleskin, etc.)   _____

Hygiene items (toothbrush, paste, floss, sanitizer, etc.) _____

Soap / body cleaning wipes / deodorant   _____

Feminine needs   _____

Self-defense (lethal or non-lethal)   _____

Duct tape   _____

Emergency cash / personal identification   _____

Maps / road atlas of surrounding areas   _____

Large trash bags   _____

Spares (batteries, bulbs, solar charger, etc.)   _____

Other _____   _____

Other _____   _____

Other _____   _____

Other _____   _____

Other _____   _____

Children's Bug-Out Bag

3 day supply of drinking water   _____

3 day supply of food   _____

Spare clothing (socks, underwear, long pants / shirt)   _____

Headlamp / flashlight and extra batteries   _____

Small first aid kit   _____

Comfort item (stuffed animal, coloring book, etc.)   _____

Other _____   _____

Rally Points / Meeting Destinations

Primary:

Location: _____

Address: _____

Phone #: _____

Contact: _____

Directions: _____

_____

_____

_____

_____

_____

Secondary:

Location: _____

Address: _____

Phone #: _____

Contact: _____

Directions: _____

_____

_____

_____

_____

Additional Notes:

I hope you've enjoyed this book and found it both useful and thought-provoking. If you would like to, check out my other book below if you are a fan of all things pertaining to the zombie apocalypse!

When The Zombie Apocalypse Comes, You're Toast....

(A Practical Guide On How Not To Become "That Guy" When Everything Goes South)

https://www.amazon.com/Zombie-Apocalypse-Comes-Youre-Toast/dp/1537043927/ref=sr_1_1?ie=UTF8&qid=1475074845&sr=8-1&keywords=shawn+clay

Feel free to connect with me on Facebook or Twitter (Shawn Clay @georgiazombies) or email me directly at the address below:

georgiazombiefighter@gmail.com